Tierce

Vaughan Pilikian

Tierce
published in the United Kingdom in 2024
by Leslie Bell T/A Mica Press & Campanula Books

47 Belle Vue Road, Wivenhoe, Colchester, Essex CO7 9LD
micapress.uk | contact@micapress.uk

ISBN 978-1-869848-3-47
Copyright © Vaughan Pilikian 2024

The right of Vaughan Pilikian to be identified as the author of this work has been asserted by him in accordance with the Copyright, Designs and Patents Act of 1988.

All rights reserved.

You hover

You hover
at the door of the world
and we watch you,
understanding nothing
of what you face,
of your life
and how it seems now to mirror
all our futures,
all our joinings and partings,
understanding nothing
of what we are, were,
one day will not be:
not daring to look away,
not daring to move,
not daring
even to breathe.

Rain fell into me

Rain fell
into me
as it fell
in the night,
as in the day it might
fall upon me,
and it chilled my blood
and I heard birds crying,
calling and crying
in the pouring rain
as they made a spiral, a chain
that flailed and failed,
unmade and remade the shape they signed,
a disintegrating line
in the sky behind
my ears, my eyes,
as they called and they cried
climbing high in the night,
climbing high
in the rain as the rain
came down
like ice in my veins,
as the rain
came down
inside me.

O the turning

O the turning,
the turning and the turning
within.
The stormsurge
that ever precedes
my rising.
In the hurricane of life
what can ever be shaped?
What can ever be made
into what it wants to be?
Who could cross
the breakingzone
and find the everunshifting
windless eye?
We glimpse it written in the splinters
on the wind,
in the dreams of our wildest despair,
in the outrage
of our trying.
We see it blindly in the night.
We know it
by all that is outside it,
by all that is,
by all, all that it is not,
by the notness
of what
never was,
never is:
by what lives
in the nevercouldbe.

Two eyes

Two eyes
that open to see one another.
Two eyelids that close
to divide.

Who is it that stirs?
Who wakes and rises?
Who gathers flowers
in the night?

I am lost
and you are lost
and I look for the way
and you look for the road
and I call to you and
you do not hear
and tears come and you do not know why
but I know why
and you call to me and
I do not hear
and you look for the road
and I look and I look
for the path.

By dustlit wasteland
I worked my fist into earth,
I opened my hand in the dark.

Tell me o tell me
because I need now to know:
what might grow
from the stone
of the heart?

Do you hear me?

Do you hear me
intone
the broken bell?

I swallowed its pieces,
I dug them from
the earth, the earth
was like
stone, the stone
was your voice, it was
calling, calling,
I clawed at the dirt.
I broke my nails on your words.

O lost country,
high and trackless,
unmarked by dreaming,
out past all the lines and the lies
on the map.

O valley
where the bell
never rang, never rang,
where neither note nor echo
was ever heard.

O daughters of the tree
who patiently
await us:
I unthroat these splinters
for you.

Comes it comes in the night

Comes it comes in the night
comes the ripple that comes
through your bones,
that rattles you
out of the deep,
that rattles you awake,
leaves you
lost, accursed,
deranged in the dark,
where nothing is as it was or ever was going to be,
where nothing will ever be
whole again,
where all is
skewed, all is
broken and breaking
and there you must dwell,
in the lostland of life,
holding fast so fast
there there you must
hold, hold
your eye astringent
and gaze against the blizzard swirling against you
and bite down and hold and bite down
horselike, blind
in the dark
bridle yourself:
they are gone long gone
they who brought you on,
and from here until forever
hosanna hosanna
from here on out you are alone.

I stand

I stand.
I stand beside the destroyed,
I stand at their shoulder,
as one of them.

I am bruised and I am broken
and that too is right.

I will live by this fury
that annihilates me
and all that is near me,
that is my birthright,
because though it consumes
only itself,
it raises high as a tattered flag
the symbol of ruination.

And though those
whom I call my brothers and sisters
will rob, batter and burn me,
still I will go
at their side,

and my idiocy
will be branded
in the black of the heavens
when I sleep.

And that,
my friends,
will be enough for me.

Glowed o glowed

Glowed o glowed,
how you sparked up
suddenly,
how you
glowed for me,
all down the dark hours
how you gleamed and glittered
and I had no rest:

I hallucinated you
through the night.

O stupor

O stupor,
and the deep deep fall.
O silence of days.
O cruelty of waking.

How many times
can I heap fuel into the flames,
how many times
close over the blaze?

In the end the fire
must consume itself:
in the end the blackened heart
must rise.

Glimpsed in night's mirror

Glimpsed in night's mirror
it seems unlikely I exist.
Frail figures pencilled in,
scratched out,
scratched in,
breathed out like mist on glass
and all the while evaporating:
well might we ask
why are we?

And the wounding hand,
and the beast of the heart
barely halfcaged in the chest,
the heat in the blood
ever rising.
How can we hold
the great web of stars
inside the closed infinity
of the skull?

What will become of all this,
become of each one of us?
Some speak of a library
burning to cinders,
others of a solar system
suddenly failing,
its planets and civilisations
undiscovered, buckling inwards,
vanishing away to dust.

A figure striking out

A figure striking out
in long grass tangled
and dark upon distant glow:
I have strayed so far

I can watch myself go,
and I know that I will not be back.
So if you pass by someone
some way from the path,

if his face seems familiar
in the day failing,
it might be best to leave him be.
He may once have been a man

akin to me, he may be
all that remains of what I once was,
or he may be nothing
of whom you think it is you see.

Twin worlds

Twin worlds
and I pass between them:
I am a pariah of both.

One was a jangle
of dreaming and loss
where I was a pale figure fumbling,
in the other only darkness
flowed and flowed
with a black wind blowing and blowing:
the walls there are oceans,
the windows suns,
the day forever going and going.

Now down the mirrorline plying
I follow the border between them.
I carry the torch
that I lit departing.
I do not know how long it will burn,
how long its twin ghosts
will be dancing and dying.

No one follows me here,
no one comes the other way:
I am alone in the gloaming.
Lighter and lighter become my steps,
stranger and quieter my roaming.

I did meet others in bygone days,
in the dimming and the dust
all enclosing.
For moments
like sparks
we shared a few things:
disbelief, bewilderment,
despair and distress.
We traded our doubt for unknowing.

A few fair pieces,
I carry them yet:
in my forgetful heart they are glowing,
like talismans polished
in fretful fingers
then held in a fist ever tightening,
their makers and purposes

lost, longlost,
but their lustre
brightening and brightening.

I hear your cries

I hear your cries
in the·fabric of the whole world:
you,
the careworn,
the heartshattered,
the everquieted.

O my people
like you I wreak the ending of all things
and I do so
alone, alone
in the slumber of the wildering haze
of my calledaway hours,
my falling.

Since you and I will never meet
I will therefore
imagine you,
imagine
my hands among your hands,
yours among mine,
given over
to all you and I will never do,
given over to break the chaos
that holds the flame
close so close
against us.

And somewhere the sun has yet to fall
staves are whittled and shaped,
crossed and uncrossed
and crossed again:
they are struck
to sound, to make
a sign, a song
for the listless,
a sign for the lost.

Unseeing or oblivious may you yet
make your way o make
your winding way
towards it:
towards
us.

At the very edge

At the very edge
of the edge:
above hell.

There are demons teeming
towards us,
all o all
is desolation.
And yet you: you know
nothing of this.

A child stands,
a tree stands,
waving in the wind:

upwards where you gaze
what remains is grazed
by the lostlight shed
by another's eyes,
a mother's eyes.

The golden leaves,
the sheaves, ashimmer,
the golden hands
open to gather.

Upraised all
in icon.

Held high, held out
beyond us.

Beset, reaved,
bereaved, bewildered:
I try to lift up my eyes,
these stones, these marbles,
to raise up my eyes,
to see what it is
you see.

O the narrowest tract

O the narrowest tract,
the hemmed
wilderness:

may you flourish,
o may you thrive.

See the brambles
rising, cresting
the fences, curving
ever higher,
see them rising
on the swathe,
see them shaped
on the green wave,
burgeoning and breaking
with life.

Fecund:
see them rise,
see them strangling the palings,
see them bluing through the dusk.

May your thistles and nettles
bristle, gnarl and twist:
thrive o thrive.

May you thrive.

That was your life

That was your life:
that mystery, passing.

Illusion that there is illusion,
that one day the prism will break,
that one day
the haze will lift,
that all will be unveiled,
that revelation will come:
you will be pulled free from the drift.

Instead odds come, ends come,
scraps and pebbles,
chips of quartz that say:
once the lightning
forged in the desert
through which you toil today.

Thirst untrammelled,
you stumble on,
you blunder
on and on.

Perhaps you gather
a handful of fragments
sharp in your fingers
that glint with a thing unnamed.

Perhaps you lose them
on your mapless journey
and start all over again.

We wake in the meander

We wake in the meander,
tumbled in the glow,
pale as ghosts
but darkening.

Do you hear me calling
from the bank of the river?
Do you see me
still standing there?
Silhouette cut
from the face of the moon.

The slow chant to chain again
the scatter of days again
comes to an end
with the end
of the dream
and we enter
one silence,
waiting
o waiting
for another.

Full of abyss
you have drunk deep
from the waters of forgetting
and yet all is vivid
and dangerous within you.

So rise now
against yourself.
Be quick.
Like they who came before you you must go,
you will have no rest.

You must turn away
and journey on.
The gates of the world will never,
will not ever,
open to you.

I belong nowhere

I belong nowhere.
Like a bird
my heart soars above the void.

Where will I find to lay my head?
Where will I end my journey,
a journey
struck forth
from a village on fire?

On fire:
fire that I took with me,
fire that was set in me.
Will I ever find a place
to douse what burns in me?

Exile
into which I was born.
My long long flight out of
what I knew,
what I did not know.
Uncrowned all
my strange starry dreams:
I am still stunned and dazzled
by the whirl
of sun to storm.

O my unresting heart carry me o carry me
with you
up, up.

I will sleep on the wing.
I will not alight.
I know the abyss below
awaits me
and I will beat out its gravity
until I can go no further,
until exhaustion
finally betrays me.

Only when at the end
I go blind and mad with weariness,
when the very last of me
is consumed
by the flames,
then and only then
will I fall.

We came here

We came here
looking for the lost,
looking o looking
for the lost.

Up in the hills,
up, up above the hills:
we climb and climb
as if to depart forever
the places we find we are
bereft.

Windfall, rainfall,
a thousand leaves
from the book of life,
gold and redgold and auburn burning:
pathway giving way to glade,
to river, to woodland,
to steep slopes,
to steppingstones.

The lost is lost within us,
the lost lost inside,
and the lost are lost in our past receding.
Can we find them again
on the winding path?
Can we seek out their steps
in our slumber?
Can we find the narrow ledge,
the narrow path to the past,
the path from the precipice
that was hidden from us?

Leaves upon leaves, falling and fallen,
leaves of our dreams,
a hundred thousand histories
cast wide to the wind.

Count o count,
count the days in which,
count the ways in which
we will not, we will never
find you,
the ways and the days
that will accumulate,
shelf upon shelf
crumbling in the blue

as we clamber and we climb
upon them,
as we climb,
as we climb on
beyond them.

To bring near the fardistant

To bring near the fardistant
as we go
into the open,
where memory can be heard
as rainfall.

How long we have waited,
in vain,
how long.

We slip back
into darkness as the day
slips away,
as the year fades away
lightly so lightly
between us.

Lodged
in the blindness
somewhere in the tracts,
in the paledaway wastelands
beneath all sunrise.

How long
we have yet to wait,
will wait, you
and
I, how
long.

Not here

Not here: not here,
but elsewhere,

just short
of forever.
Remembering how to forget again,
how to be
forgotten.

Dwindling: flickering
and rising.
Like a candle
burning in reverse.

Venus.
Pale fissile jade
in the breadth above.
What is it that you bring to me?
Smooth and cold
as a stone in the palm.

And higher yet:
a single unnamed star,
vastly alone,
shimmering out,
soon to vanish again
into the haze.

Beheld for this moment,
celestial:

and mine
the two eyes
to see you both.

Some strange night fire

Some strange
night fire,
very cold,
torments me.

Half-
drowned
in the terror and the wonder
I ask:

can I yet
anchor myself

to you?
Can you pull me back?

O miracle.
So far:
never further.

How the distance between us
fills us.

Lamplight so cautious,
held forth,
trembling,

if only to try
to imagine you by.

I drift on,
the dark swell
somewhere beneath,

with dust of blackened suns
falling all around.

In secret
I will whisper
into the shell of my hand
the neverhope

that you
will not,
ever not

hear me.

Emerging snowblind

Emerging snowblind
in the violent winter.

Setting out
cleaving to the rumour
of the slowly
climbing
eye of the day.

Fullzoned
in whiteness.
Was it a voice,
calling to you, calling to me?
The wind
whipped away the words
as soon as our mouths had made them.

Long downgoing
into wild silence:
we drop the spears of night
into the drifts,
hoping to forget
we ever held them,
hoping one day
to return this way,
to chance another time
upon them.

Smears,
beastmade,
on the sometime sky.

Circles
spun wide
in the unperimetered.

To see through
the icelantern.

To watch
for infractions
in the nothingness.

Like the wolves
who weave our horizon
we go where the firelight fades.

In the vestibule

In the vestibule
between disguises,
cut through
by floodlamps.
Did you know then
this moment was to be our last?
Did you know
you would never see me again?

Two figures,
shadows of themselves,
shadows of one another.
The antechamber.
We stepped aside
to let night flow suddenly through us.

Twin cones,
worldlines swept out at the points,
twin horizons
hourglasslike
within which we were set by time
across each other.

Riverside.
In between wonders
the circle closing
becomes a helix.
All things deceive in the continuum
except light,
which now fades.

Eyes gleaming,
lips moving:
red, black, red.
A hand brushed
by a hand.
Words to echo my words.
You grow darker and fainter
as I watch you disappear.

I know little
of what became of you.
I followed
the narrow line
scored through the immensity
that flickered around me
and here is where I came to.
Strange
how you haunt me even now.
Stranger yet
all that was to come.

The tree shivers
greengold,
illuminated after the rain.
You are here with me in the morning
but soon you will be gone.

I cannot solve the riddle of you.
I can make no sense
of what it was
we never were.

Your breath alone

Your breath alone
is how you are,
and it leaves no mark
upon the world.

It is given
and recalled
and given again,
sent forth
with the falling of your chest,
drawn back in its rise.

You are the breathing one,
the one across whom
life ripples mysteriously
in the shift from foot to foot,
the sigh, the hand at the neck,
the glance, the dance
of the eye.

Like peacocks and orchids
you are set here
to bewitch others with your being,
so miraculous, so haughty,
so odd, inimitable,
and so brief:
so soon gone.

I want no roof above my head

I want no roof above my head
no walls
to hold out the weather.
I do not crave
the heat of the hearth,
no quilt of down or feather.

No shutters or blinds
can banish the sky
that calls upon us,
that summons us.
No windows or doors can close out the night
that rises and rises within us.

So take my coat
that it may keep you warm,
take my shoes to remind you of me:
sharp may the pebbles be
beneath my bare feet.
I want only the storm and the stars.

Dreamer of the dream whoever you are:
I will be your somnambulist.
As I journey towards you engulf me,
consume me forever
in the black ice cold
of your supernal snowlike fire.

Resplendent

Resplendent
in the high reaches
where the night meets
the concrete and mirrorglass
suspended above us:

thrown through them,
fetched up
across them.

Your face is occluded in halfdarkness,
your hands are prayer hands
aped against heaven.

Black smoke curling,
cupped
from the senses
awoken
in the drummed out
intervals
between us.

Traveller all tattered
and awry, unsung.
Roadgoer,
dry field dust
on your shoulders.

I take your scarlet snakescales
and curl them
knifesharp
under my tongue

and I hold you
before me:
unyielding,
unrelenting in the turning of things
and rising ever rising
like the sun.

My steed came past

My steed came past
steep as thunder,
I tried to grab it,
I slipped and scrambled in the whites of its eyes
as they rolled up
into my head.
It was wild,

it bucked beneath
my hand, my hand
went through the cool flame of its mane
as if it went through water,
hooves clattering,
its mad snorts
clobbered and crowned me:
some raddled my ears,
some swam unheard above my head,
some stormed and rippled
in my mouth.
I saw the marks

upon its flanks,
I saw its marks upon me and for a moment
as my teeth bit steel
I wondered vainly
if I might be its master,
or if I might once
have been going to be.

Wild it was, and untamed,
and it galloped on
and it was gone.

It left me blinking in the mud and dust,
as if it had never been,
as if I
had never been.

O the breach

O the breach:
to break through,
to reach the gold
in the broken,
the course of otherwise,
pulse of the whatcanbe,
the whatcouldbe,
spilled in the yoke.

O unshouldering,
unsplinting,
overthrowing, overturning
of you and I,
of how you and I might be
unmade, unarrayed,
might be made again.

O the brokenover,
the trodden
down, smashed
down, down,
rammed down in the gutter.

O codex of stars
lying open in the day,
etched and stuttered
blindinlaid signs of all
that has not come to pass,
that will never be
nor ever
be reborn to be
the yettocome.

O shadowbright the bounty
on the tree that grows
uprooted, down
into earth,
into night below,
and cold the pale sun
in the springs beneath.

All that unmirrors what is:
I will never cease
to dream of you.

You came running at me

You came
running at me
and I spread my arms to catch you
and we
tipped over the brink
into freefall: the world

turned over
and over
as we fell, as we
turned over the world,
over each other. I saw the diamonds
hammered into heaven
filing in your eyes,
I saw the mandorlas
opening,
I saw us falling and falling
through them,
I saw how perhaps we then could see
what chaos might be
in the mind of its maker.

If you were afraid
I would never have known it
though I heard
your cry
in the long milky trails
smeared out
across the rapturous blue ascending

as we came apart
for the last time,
as we

tumbled on alone,
you and I,
as we tumbled deeper ever deeper
into the open,

into the unfathomable,
on o on:
on.

Life, life

Life, life:
I knew you once.
I will find my way back to you
before you cast me out forever
into the dark
from which I have come.

These tricks and traps,
these demons and dreams,

shifting shadows
of what I thought I was:
these twisting ways, these snarled paths,
pondered, longwandered,
winding back
upon themselves,
upon places
I may have known in passing,
places in passing
I may have made my own
though name them I can none.

Walking, wondering,
meandering, stumbling.

How much further do I have to go?
How much of my journey is done?
What more will be given
and what will be taken?
Why this trial
in the eye of the sun?

Hold out for me

Hold out for me, hold out:
there is a thing that goes from me to you,
there is a thing
that transcribes
our diastance.

It goes out
in the night.
Sent forth,
lit up wildly:
like a bird plumed in moonlight
with the brush of a wingtip
it touches the very lip of the impossible,
and circles back around
to return.

Wait for it
in the bright field of morning.
Wait for it to swing down
even now
and alight and cling
to the crook
of your upraised hand.

O the streams

O the streams
let loose
from above you,
pouring down upon me,
down upon my face
and through my hands.
O the hailstones of your eyes
drumming on mine,
drumming o drumming
on mine.
When I wake I return
to dreams to dream
how once long ago
I bathed in your rain,
how I dived in and swam and froze
in your streams,
how they gushed in upon me,
how they swirled
and billowed,
flooded up around me,
lashed and caressed me:
how they
broke me apart,
made me whole.

Tonight the daughters of Perseus

Tonight the daughters of Perseus
will fall:
they will streak the sky
like tears.
I will not wait nor will I watch for them.
Into the deep
I go after you:
I will not make you mine.
In luminous brine
with the seashoals and the krill,
among eyelets in myriad
I will lose you.
I will find you a thousand times.
I will lose you a thousand more.
All I know is the cold,
the vast and shimmering
blackness.
Diving down dumbly I will seek you
there and there
somewhere
I will find you,
my pale pearlblue star.
I will prise you free
and you will drift away
through my fingers.
I will lose you in the force of the swell.

Might it be?

Might it be
that I pass through you,
that you
pass through me?
A gateway,
eyes rolled heavenward:
all along our milkwhite rivers
to the place of scars and ruin,
the origin of all journeys.

Drunk in the garden:
we have not yet even set out
and the sun is already gone.
Later, in a lost hour,
I find it again somehow crammed within you,
bursting your narrow seams.
I swallow it whole.

O strand of they that have come before us,
coil twisted, spiraldrilling
auger through the passage of light
from mouth to mouth,
tongue to tongue.

The sounds do not match,
do not transpose.
We live in the silence of your scrying down,
its depthlessness.
Will we ever speak again?
Our voices will give out beneath us.
We are weightless,
never forgiven,
floating, falling.

Many years to go by
with dreams collapsing.
I know I will live through them all.

Like a drowning man,
ambivalent,
loosening his hold on life,
surrendering
the breath in his lungs,
gulping it back.

Lip to head to hand to mouth
to hand: thumb, from eye
to eye.

Halting now,
reaching for the unspoken,
reaching, quietly, desperately
and yet there
at the shifting centre,
locked against us:

the void, starless,
where the word might even so,
even yet,
might somehow
come to be.

I will look up

I will look up,
up through
the narrowest window,

I will find an opening,
embrasure of sky,
trees, jitter of birds,
autumn leaves to sweep me

on and over
the bridge of night,
to sign me past the heavenly snares,

lead me through
the adjacency of ruins
crumbled
and toppled
around me.

And I will look out from inside
with no greater vision
than my eyes can afford,
no greater heart
than the one
somehow knotted
and set beating in my chest.

And I will make ready to go forth
when the time comes,
when all that
is is
turned to what is not,
all that is not
turned again to what is,

when the walls
are no more,
when the doors are no more,

when at last
we are free
as none ever were free,
as we never
dared dream
we might be.

Perhaps it was you

Perhaps it was you:
perhaps, perhaps
it was you.

Perhaps it was you I saw
travelling towards me
down days now past,
travelling away
down the days hence.

Perhaps it was you I followed
back towards what I thought was to come,
on towards
what was gone.

Perhaps it was you who pushed into my hand
blue ice tears
I clutched at until they were no more,
who left me stray messages
sparking and spinning:
patterns paling
in the dusk.

Perhaps it was you who came
slipping like a sylph through my sleep
before I could close the gap
in time and distance
that would take me on towards you,
that would take me
back and away.

Perhaps it was you for whom
I rang out all the bells between heaven and earth.
Perhaps it was you who heard me.

O perhaps, perhaps
it was you.

To reach out

To reach out
into emptiness,
into echoless space.

To fling out
the rope of whispers,
breathbraided,
that it might somehow catch
on the unsayable.

Into the opening
over the gulf:
the drop,
vaster and vaster.

To strike out
far, far
beneath
the stuff of the stars.

To hang somehow
in between nothings.

To be the firsttime lasttime
funambulist,

swinging wider and wider
above the chasm,

wondering
at the mystery
of what yet suspends him,

doubling up with laughter
at his folly.

For fevered hours

For fevered hours
we pursued one another,
we chased one another
down the empty walkways
that crossed and crisscrossed
the voids
built into us.

We went past each other,
we doubled back.

In the waste below
we were wounded things,
we prowled and loped and circled each other:
we went in and out
of shadow and scrub
and as the angles proliferated
between us
we broke blind
across our own frontiers.

Reaving the halfdemolished wonderland
I saw you fray through the neon:
as you fugued
in the spirit fumes
I heard faraway concussions
rhythm the night.

I sent my hummingbirds
up through your throat.

You buried your moonstones
in my eyes.

I came crashing into your glades

I came crashing
into your glades and clearings
where the wild creatures of your troubled halfsleep
frolicked and fought.

In frenzy
I flailed in the distance
that opened the tunnels between
two words for world,
where a lost language
wove the spells together.

Travesty
and tumult.
I twisted in the long courses of purest moonlight
running from the gush
of your and my
inrushing
breath

and I stole down
the narrow tracks you made,
you carved in red
with your fingernails.

Soon I knew
all the voices of all those
who had struggled for supremacy within you,
with flash of tooth and eye
cut you down.

I gathered what was left of you:
lustre of the darkly made.
And everything fell
and fell forever.

I took your ruin
into me,
immensely:

I drove on through you
with my own.

In the sheer cerulean

In the sheer cerulean,
cut wide,
violent and pure,
the bird made of sky
took flight
and was gone.

All that remains
here on earth
is a brass rubbing
of the thing
we once
called life.

To be like the foxes

To be like the foxes,
glimpsed in repose,
sleeping faunlike through the afternoon,
seeping through time:
fire brackets
curled upon themselves,
upon unreadable secrets,
hunched with heat
then stretched out and oblivious,
starting at the flight of a bird,
a change in the wind,
gone when I come near,
soundlessly, gone, gone
into the dusk, gone
into the yellow moon,
and now cold, roaming, abroad,
at nightwork,
silent and sinuous as the clouds go indigo,
then spouting and barking
somewhere at the dark
and come the sunrise
as likely to return again and be glimpsed again
as not, as never to be back.

O to have such power,
such might.
To be all aflame, all wildfire.
To flare through the flow of life,
a dream struck from a dream.

And if we split the earth

And if we split the earth
you and I,
if we fell,
feeling the icebergs of the night
near enough to crush us to
a whisper, the whisper
we set quivering
between two hands
like a dove
cupped close to your chest,

then decades will pass,
will give way and crumble,
they will
pass, pass
and come to nothing.

But that fault,
the schism,
will run corrupting
through our hearts,
through our hearts and beneath them,
will run through the years,
through the labyrinthine streets,
the edgelands and the fields,
through the roots and the stems of flowers
bursting forth
and wilting and dying to dust
and the trunks of trees with their leaves
budding and unwrapping and green and gone grey,
all the generations and disintegrations
and the clocks
wound, wound down
and wound again,

until with neither warning nor sign
the day will come,
the hour, the minute,
when we will pass by one other once again,
you and I:
the long circumference will close,
casual as dreamers we will pass
within inches
of breath,
of touch,
we will meet once more
at the rift
and we will not speak
and I will not look
at you
and you
will not look at me

and on the other side of the world
the coral will bloom
beneath the sea.

In the slaughterhouse of time

In the slaughterhouse of time
I try to speak to you
in gouts,
mouthing and miming
until the halfshaped words
liquefy
and slide away
or dry up and blow away
and when they are gone I listen:
it is like drinking fire through my ears,
the smoke
thickens and thickens about us,
and the slow forking of years
grows vinelike
and wraps around our throats,
unjoints us,
our burning limbs
prised one from the other,
embrace of serpents
binding at the neck,
wrist pressed to wrist as if to transfuse
the very flow of the
heart, hands
arching apart,
your pulse steals mine,
draws it up and away down the decades
until slumbrous,
rolling over,
you press yourself
into the soft clay
of the river
that parts suddenly
in the halfheld secrets of the blood.

Songs, songs

Songs, songs
to ring out in another time,
a time to come,
a time
that was once
and never again will be.
Here,
where
their
words
are not heard,
let us cup to our ears
the silence
that brings the dream of them
as the shell
brings the sound
of the sea.

We are destroyed again and again

We are destroyed again and again,
our lives
destroyed,
our words are lost,
our books and our chronicles
are drowned in the earth
as our mothers and fathers
were drowned in time.

We are steeped in the mud
that will not take us,
we are deep in corruption and decay:
the streaming white sunless
growth of the underworld
ropes and binds us,
it binds our limbs,
thrashing and flailing to be free.

I know you, I knew you, you were she
that raised me,
and you: you as a child
were the man I was to be

and the roof ripped off, fire doused, mare and nightmare

coming down the generations,
coming down the twisted braid,

mare riding nightmare,
nightmare riding mare,

galloping on across the border between hell and home,

galloping in
through the wall
where the house is gone,
where only the hearth still stands,

a monolith,
its brick throat
mute and cold as the throats of they who were
forced to eat stones, as the
voiceless lie waiting, as the
soundless
lie down
in frenzy.

We wake and we sleep
and we wake
again and when
we wake again
we will begin again,
we will return to our ending to live again,
to die again,
to live again.

Somehow you saw into me

for C

Somehow you saw into me
You took my damage
from me,
beheld it safely
in your arms
even as time laid waste to you,
worked in secret
to steal you away.

How many I wonder can say the same?
You were the shuttle
that wove us,
you saw the warp and the weft
between us,
and we cohered briefly on your loom as you left us
and then
to be true to you we few
came apart
once again.

All was always collapsing
but you shook us free from gravity.

As others wept or wailed you went among the stones,
swept them up, juggled them in air,
struck them together, made sparks, turned rocks
into apples and tossed them
into our hands:
you raised a gentle flame
all through our listless days
to light up
our etchedaway nights.

Gift of gifts,
benison,
manna in the heart:
as rich and pure
as it must evanesce.

Your quiet beguiling,
your flint and grace
are gone now,
your delicate arms,
gone,
and your beholding,
gone forever,
held in earthlight.

We were strangers, we became friends.
Did I return even a fraction of your kindness?
I will never know.

As we were made,
quick and sudden,
and as we crossed paths,
in mystery:
so even so
are we sundered.

A kind of knowledge

A kind of knowledge
that consumes us,
that bursts into being as we do,
then one day
winks out,
and hard it is
to forgive or comprehend
a universe that places with its glittering nebulae
demise inside your head
that I now press to my mine,
orb to orb,
the death of the flowering earth,
the collapse and end of the sun
and of all living things that are and are yet to be,
and you must grow
and tremble and laugh through these realisations
with my feeble hand on the helm as the ship
lists and disintegrates:
for I can hold
nothing, nothing
but you, I can be nothing
but a desperate sign for you
glimpsed between peaks in the leagues
and leagues of wild waste,
and the love that is in us will break us whole,
the gifts are too great,
they scatter beyond us,
too precious
all the spoils of darkness.

And yet hush:
still, still
somehow
you press more
into me,
into my inmost core
than the universe can hold
or entropy
ever undo.

Eyes hidden

Eyes hidden
he floats in peace,
set to sleep in a steel bowl,
wreathed in fuchsia and rose:
the wordless one,
the infant.

You who placed him there sleep too,
you who know you are
somehow his kin,
and though you recognise yourself in him even so
you have learned to cross barriers alone,
to cross streams
as all creatures must,
as we cross oftentimes to you,
swaying in the current, uncertain,
and you have perhaps left him as a message to me
upon the opposite bank,
returning late, alone,
an absence that perhaps brushed lightly
against your sublime unconcern.

I see your hand in the trace
and pattern of his display:
enrobed in blue as if
wrapped in sky
or water, adrift, gone
for now in his own
breathless way as you
are breathing gone,

as I too might yet find release
from the fury of midnight's ardour
into who could imagine
what impossible dreamings,
bodying forth
what impossible worlds,
myths for the morning's
fragmentary retelling, though it will be for you
to hazard even the barest details
of where your silent companion will have spent
these hours to come, what wonders he saw through them,
his dollseyes alone of all of ours
swayed and kept stable by the tilt of the pure earth,
its lucent magic:

by gravity, which the rest of us seem
in our sudden jolts and awakenings
desperately to believe
by some arcane mechanism
hidden in our hearts
we might somehow defy.

That light flows

That light flows,
that it burns at the edges with all else dark,
that it makes sacred,

that unseen in the hollow
the ivy and sycamore
entwine,

that others fall across us
like seeds, like snowflakes, scattering and melting,
that you are you,
you and no one else,
like others but not quite the same,

that I do not know you, that I will never
know you, that the birdflight
comes in low, thud of wings, pulse in the dimming,
releasing us, telling us
of another way, another place,

that you walked out of the house,
that you entered the ocean
a fledgling, a tiny thing,
that the ocean entered you,
a glittering vastness,
that you dreamt of drowning,
that you feared it, fell into it,
wished for where the waves would go,
that the waves went where you wished they would,

that pomegranates and apples will grow ripe,
some for us, but most
not for us,
that all things blossom and fall and blossom
and fall,
that blossom flutters as it falls,

that it all goes, it goes and it was nothing
and it was for nothing,

that these few words might hold all of this,
some of this,
almost, if only
for a time.

All gentleness

All gentleness
runs with your wild beasts,
since they have taught your fierceness
to be kind.

Dragonrider,
tamer of wolves and wyverns,
if you destroy you do so
only to raise up the palaces
hidden between
the sheets of the wind
so that we might stroll through storied rooms
and climb the spiral stairs
above the clouds.

You have opened me.
You have
the light I lost, the light that left me
and passed to you
and passed through you back
into all that is.
Now you gather it again to yourself
effortlessly,
clasp it pressed in your hand
like a nugget of gold
swept from the broadflowing stream.

You hold it there: the glimmer.
You.
You hold it for us, for the frozen

and the fallen,
the failing, the fading,
the givenway, the fractured, the foundered.
You hold it
for each of us,
for every one of us, first to last:
upon your palm
are written in full flame
all our worn and faded names.

Let me stay near you then
o magus
of the straitened ways,
bookless scholar,
seer of the spangled air.
Let me remain with you o let me stay
long enough
that I might learn my life
by heart again,
that I might start again
from wherever it was
I left off.

This is the secret

This is the secret
you were never told:
everything carries you out of yourself
and drives you back inside.
You will be ruptured
and break
and mend again and break again
and mend again
and nothing
will remain, all will accrue and fray
and fade away,
all accumulate, out of reach,
and whispering to yourself in the dark of the day
you will beg in the light of the night
for what you once cast aside,
and in search of stillness you will come upon
cacophony,
in search of openness
enclosure,
and you will cease to breathe
and somehow find air in the crevices
between and between:
nothing will be as you feared it would be,
nothing will be
as you dreamt it might.
And all the questions you raised
as a child
to the starry sky
will fall again upon you
like flakes of unearthly snow,
one by one:
each intact, exquisite, unanswered.

O teeming world

O teeming world
take me with you,
let me into you.
I will go up as you go up,
I will burst forth
into the day,
I will break with you
into flight and blossom.
My eyes I give
to your myriad,
my arms and legs to your crux and jointing,
my head to your avalanche,
my feet to your tundra,
My blood will be your resin and your nectar,
my bones your luminescence.
My nerves and veins
will be your rivers and trees,
and the wind flowing through them
my thoughts
spun clear.
The clay of my cares
will be no more,
the tangles and prayers and the desperations
all swept away.
I will join with you:
your rage
and abeyance
will build
and break in me.
O take me up, take me into you.
Undo me.

And we too

And we too,
we will wrestle with gods:

in parkinglots gangled over with weeds,
in roadways leading nowhere,
in grey abandoned rooms
we will battle and fall
like warriors of old,
our names swallowed up
in the mouth of time.

In the blind corners and the dead ends,
in the boardedup cells,
the narrow kennels,
the spoiled cages,
in the fencedoff places forgotten to the world
we will traffic with angels,
hear words in no human tongue:
we will be gifted secrets
stolen from those that roved and raged
these solitary ways
before us.

And thus instructed,
with our fingers we will in visions
trace the interlocking glyphs
chiselled above the high door of heaven:
we will learn how to journey out
past all we have known.
Eyes rapid and reeling,
closed fast against the dark,
we will be given to see how our prison is made,
the pillars into earth,
how we might slip
unnoticed
between them.

We will trade ourselves for all that is most distant.
The horizon without
will be the horizon within.
When we arch our backs our spines will be bows
and our volleys
will darken the sun.
When we dip our heads in the poison rivers
our skulls will be grails
and the profaned waters
once again run pure.

Into the rockpools of our ears
the wandering sirens all wasted away
will pour
their unheard yearning.
We will keep their longing safe,
invite them to come
to destroy themselves
with us,
upon us.

Paper trumpets,
bent thimbles,
keys, string, dice and dust:
these will be the regalia of our banishment,
the symbols of our triumphant
returning.

And when the day breaks
across our unyielding crowns,
even as the manacles and chains are put upon us,
we will hold near what seems lost
in shadows, glimpses,
sudden alignments:
wisps and shreds of the majesty
that once was ours
will drift yet
in aura
among us.

Everything is written

Everything is written
in the breviary
of the night:
it begins and ends
all unread,
unspoken
in the swirling script
on its whispering
leaves, leaves

from the tree
that I called by your name,
in whose shade
I sheltered
from the sun,
from the rain,
and among whose roots
I buried my voice
years ago,

and at the dawn to come,
as at every dawn since,
I will listen
to the liturgy
of the starlings
and the dandelions
that have found
in you
their home.

O dove

O dove.
O bird of my heart,
I release you:
go free,
go free.

I set you forth
into the limitless.
O spread your fine rippling wings
and soar.

O fly,
fly to the walls of the world,
then fly higher,
fly over, fly past them,
let them vanish beneath you,
let them vanish
behind you,
vanish from your memory
as if they never were.

Fly far
into brightness.
With the blades of your feathers
divide the clouds,
sing through the white hallucinating fire
beyond them.
May the marvels you find
on your way
be myriad,
safe your flight
through the wonder.

O my dove: fly.
These wisps of your down
will be my keepsakes,
these fledging clawmarks
upon my arms,

and in lonely times
I will recall the fragile tremble of your life
against my hand.

I was breathed out

I was

breathed out
from the mouth of the god with the twisted horns,

fluttering like filigree
I was flung forth and now further I fly
across the curve of the hill above the valley,
the deep slope
roping into cold
and frayed away and laved
by the scurfing grey waves
of an alien sea.

Flowing above I am a river in air:
I warp and spring
the bracing of the world,
turning it liquid around me.
Struck low by the herd I was
forced aside,
driven outward, run wide:
now my tracks are eccentric
and radiant the sparks
at my hooves.
They say death
seeks out the outcast.
But we are all
so very far from the savannah that made our kind.

O you who do not know me

I have been the exile and I have shared with my brothers
the noonday feast.
They will not shelter me again.
I vaulted the pen and now
I run alone: now
I sense the dusk
dropping on my back
but I do not stop.
I arch outward,
past all borders,
I make my way through time and the turning
lantern of shadows,
endless through days I and no other ever will number:
my life is a cry of wonder unheard.

I sing on
through the collapsing light
the cascades of all tomorrow.
High up
in solitude
one word alone
can leap with me,
can cross with me

from sunbeam through shade to shade and back to sun,
one word only:

antelope.

What are you?

What are you?
Tangled here, erupting:
bloodcourse,
seedcarrier,
whethervane.
Halfswung from the circuit of things,
half outside,

half inside:
worlddenier,
lost to yourself.
Twisted in then torn out,
tightspiralling,
unspooling,
a rope of liquid pearls
is all that
suspends you,

binds you in falling.
Watch now
the circle of your time
diminishing.
Only in the gap between two breaths
can you and I
be glimpsed.

My life is a fever

My life is a fever,
nothing in it remains:
all goes astray,
all wild and wildweary,
all sheers away in the stream.

I clove through to you,
through the frost of the forest
I came cleaving
through the trees.
I cut clear a path:

in delirium I came,
into oblivion I pass.

I pass on and all fades,
the clearings I made
decay into thickets,
mere figments we seem,
we are gone in a day:

all there is,
all there was
frays, fails away
in the surge, strain and sway
of the dream.

The broken

The broken,
only the broken:
the broken are the ones
who will climb.

They will climb
from the pit
into which they were thrown,
they will find a way back
and they will climb
to the heights,
they will leave all the rest of us
behind.

Mephitic in the gutter,
laid low against the stone,
at the mouth of the underground
you slumber:
on one hand a lotus,
on one hand an owl,

arms scored radiant
with tracks carved for paradise,
fingernails split yellow from scrabbling
at the filthcaked corners
of unforgettable days.

A tattooed teardrop
blues the corner of your eye
but tantalising sleep
will banish it for now.

The wornaway pillow
now falls away,
the loaf crumbles away
into your lap.

O climb, climb:
climb the golden ladder
the angels of oblivion
let down now
before you.
Leave us all here,
leave us behind:
leave us
heartless, mindless, confined.

To know

To know
by the breath within you,
the heat in the blood,
that this is not who we are,
not what we are.
To know by the distance we have come,
by the distance
we have yet to go,
by the measure
reasoned in the tread
of our days and our nights,
by the songs
frozen in our birthlines,
the ferocity in the chest,
lightning in the arms,
the fingers wrought from our palms,
the cordings of throat and thigh,
the thud and sinew
rhythmed within us.
We are not
how we seem to be
nor what we might become:
we are only how it is
we ever were.

Like you

Like you
I am alone
and like you
were I not I would not
have to find a way
to speak
these words, these few words,
fewer yet,
these words, like you,
that were not
ever yet
and never will
be mine.

It is the blue glister of your eyes

It is the blue glister of your eyes:
I have seen it before
and I have seen the blue meadows
broken across them
and the blue just as bright
of the sky,
metamorphic and broad
and borderless above them.
I too might imagine where you are bound.

May this be the yearning
from which we all might learn
rumour of some narrow crossing
back through us,
clear past the twists
and the tortures
we have wound and wound in
around us.

Old wanderer lashed by the elements,
tatterdemalion,
wrapped in patchwork against the dark of the year,
clad amber, goldgrey and dusty rose:
you draw down the sun,
send it rolling
in the hurtle of shadows
that we might rise at its fall,
might rise
and set forth
beneath you.

Your hands once scales to weigh
shame against charity,
palms up upon the pavement,
will now gather in our griefs,
crumble them to dust.
Unburdened
we will leave this land
of violence and ruin,
vow ourselves
with you
into the beyond.

Hemmed at the heart with oaths,
hoarse from crying to the distance,
damaged but unbowed
we will heave the sea about us behind us:
we will be
your oarsmen,
your acolytes,
your tribe.

O crippled prophet
crushed in the brow,
doused in spirit
and drowsing.
Upraise your clarion, call us forth.
We will light out with you,
we will breach the horizon and journey on through.
We will seek our lost home
in the heights.

O starflake

O starflake,
everdiffering:
your millionyear odyssey
has come
to an end.

Carried here
on solar winds
through the unencompassable,
on the brightest of nights

you have fallen
into me: into me
and far,
so very very far
from forever.

I will raise my heathen words

I will raise
my heathen words
up into heaven:
I will not leave them here.

I will sink
steeped in the starlit mire:
battling for scraps
with the starved and the sunstruck
I will come to nothing
and go to nothing.

But you,
winged things,
flutterers, deceivers,
dreamstuff
on such as which I was never made,
fripperies and lies
and halftruths, chipped and speckled
earthpieces,
like bits of stone or glass
cast up and cast apart
I will send you up,
ever higher,
up.

I will strew you to be lost
flaring in the glory
across the opening and opening
of the sky,
where no one goes,
no one breathes,
no one: where no one
may ever more
listen.

You slung the javelins

You slung the javelins
of madness and yearning
deep o deep
within me,

shafts cut
from the trees of Eden,
whittled with the steel
of our doubled hands:
how deep,
and with what demented force,

and still they fall
and I listen and wait
and still
they fall, they fall.

How few the days

How few the days,
how brief the hours,
how little remains
yet to be.

O poverty take
these things from my hands,
tear them away,
set me free:

that I might craft
with nothing,
that nothing
might craft with me.

Index

A figure striking out, 11
A kind of knowledge, 68
All gentleness, 74
And if we split the earth, 60
And we too, 78
At the very edge, 16
Comes it comes in the night, 6
Do you hear me? 5
Everything is written, 81
Emerging snowblind, 30
Eyes hidden, 70
For fevered hours, 55
Glimpsed in night's mirror, 10
Glowed o glowed, 8
Hold out for me, 45
How few the days, 97
I belong nowhere, 37
I came crashing into your glades, 56
I hear your cries, 14
I stand, 7
I want no roof above my head, 35
I was breathed out, 84
I will look up, 50
I will raise my heathen words, 95
In the sheer cerulean, 58
In the slaughterhouse of time, 62
In the vestibule, 32
It is the blue glister of your eyes, 92
Life, life, 44
Like you, 91
Might it be? 48
My life is a fever, 87
My steed came past, 38

Not here, 27
O dove, 82
O starflake, 94
O stupor, 9
O teeming world, 77
O the breach, 40
O the narrowest tract, 18
O the streams, 46
O the turning, 3
Perhaps it was you, 52
Rain fell into me, 2
Resplendent, 36
Some strange night fire, 28
Somehow you saw into me, 66
Songs, songs, 63
That light flows, 72
That was your life, 19
The broken, 88
This is the secret, 76
To be like the foxes, 59
To bring near the fardistant, 26
To know, 90
To reach out, 54
Tonight the daughters of Perseus, 47
Twin worlds, 12
Two eyes, 4
We are destroyed again and again, 64
We came here, 24
We wake in the meander, 20
What are you? 86
You came running at me, 42
You hover, 1
You slung the javelins, 96
Your breath alone, 34

Milton Keynes UK
Ingram Content Group UK Ltd.
UKHW051140070724
445121UK00006B/46